COME TO MY FADEN

Eastern Catholics in the United States of America is a work of the Committee on the Relationship between Eastern and Latin Catholic Churches and is an adaptation of an original publication by the Australian Catholic Bishops' Conference entitled *Eastern Catholics in Australia*, published in 1997 (ISBN 1-86420-112-6). Permission for the adaptation was given by the Australian Catholic Bishops' Conference. This work was approved as a publication of the Committee on the Relationship between Eastern and Latin Catholic Churches by the Administrative Committee of the National Conference of Catholic Bishops in March 1999 and is authorized for publication by the undersigned.

Msgr. Dennis M. Schnurr
General Secretary, NCCB/USCC

Icon of Christ the Teacher by Alexandre Moscalionov. Icons depict the presence of the person portrayed. This icon depicts the aspect of Christ as a teacher showing us the way to live our lives. Some Eastern Catholics receive the Sacrament of Penance in the presence of this icon.

ISBN 1-57455-287-2

First Printing, June 1999

The Church as a Mystery

In its *Dogmatic Constitution on the Church*, the Second Vatican Ecumenical Council described the nature of the Church and its encompassing mission.[1]

Vatican II described the Church as a mystery. It is, as Pope Paul VI said, "a reality imbued with the hidden presence of God."[2]

"The mystery of the holy Church is already brought to light in the way it was founded. For the Lord Jesus inaugurated his Church by preaching the Good News, that is, the coming of the kingdom of God. . . ."[3]

"Vatican II situated the mystery of the Church in the mystery of God's wisdom and goodness which draws the whole human family and indeed the whole of creation into unity with God. To this end God sent into the world Jesus, born of Mary the Virgin, who was raised up on the cross, entered into glory and poured out the Holy Spirit through whom He calls and draws into unity of faith, hope and love the people of the new Covenant which is the Church."[4]

The Church as Community

"In order to establish his Church in every place until the end of the ages, Christ entrusted to the college of the Twelve to which He chose Peter as head of the office of teaching, sanctifying and governing the Church."[5] Vatican II presents the Church as the new People of God, uniting in itself, in all the richness of their diversity, men and women from all nations and all cultures.[6]

"Catholics hold the firm conviction that the one Church of Christ subsists in the Catholic Church 'which is governed by the successor of Peter and by the bishops in communion with him.'"[7]

We "confess that the entirety of revealed truth, of sacraments, and of ministry that Christ gave for the building up of his Church and the carrying out of its mission is found within the Catholic communion of the Church."[8]

The Church: A Communion of Churches

The Universal Catholic Church is, as Vatican II taught, "a corporate body of Churches."[9] It "is made up of the faithful who are organically united in the Holy Spirit by the same faith, the same sacraments and the same government. They combine into different groups, which are held together by their hierarchy, and so form particular churches or rites."[10]

The Universal Church traditionally has been divided into "East" and "West." These terms "have acquired a very precise meaning in ecclesiastical language, in which they are used with reference to the division of the Roman Empire, introduced by Diocletian at the end of the third century and which became definitive at the death of Theodosius.

"Ecclesiastically, the Western (and Latin) territories, together with the faithful who reside there, are those which were formerly part of the Western Roman Empire and those which received Christianity from these countries. Eastern territories are those which were formally part of the Eastern Roman Empire, and a few others situated beyond the Eastern boundaries of the Empire, together with their faithful and those others who received Christianity from them."[11]

There are four original Eastern traditions: Antiochian, Alexandrian, Byzantine, and Armenian.

The four of these can be further subdivided into the following Catholic Churches:

Antiochian: West Syrian (Syro-Antiochian, Maronite, and Malankarese Churches) and East Syrian (Chaldean and Malabarese Churches);

Alexandrian: Coptic and Ethiopian Churches;

Byzantine: These Churches originate from the Byzantine tradition: Albanian, Belarusan, Bulgarian, Croatian, Czech, Greek, Hungarian, Italo-Greek, Melkite, Romanian, Russian, Ruthenian, Slovak, Ukrainian.

Armenian: The Armenian Church.

We have been accustomed to speaking of the Latin (Roman or Western) Rite or the Eastern Rites to designate these different Churches. However, the Church's contemporary legislation as contained in the *Code of Canon Law* and the *Code of Canons of the Eastern Churches* makes it clear that we ought to speak not of rites, but of Churches. Canon 112 of the *Code of Canon Law* uses the phrase "autonomous ritual Churches" to designate the various Churches.

According to Vatican II, the development of these Churches was part of God's plan. "It has come about through divine providence that, in the course of time, different Churches set up in various places by the apostles and their successors joined together in a multiplicity of organically united groups which, whilst safeguarding the unity of faith and the unique divine structure of the universal Church, have their own discipline, enjoy their own liturgical usage and inherit a theological and spiritual patrimony."[12]

Concerning the Eastern Churches, Vatican II said that "Provision must be made therefore everywhere in the world to protect and advance all these individual churches."[13]

In his apostolic letter *Orientale Lumen* of May 2, 1995, Pope John Paul II said that a "conversion is . . . required of the Latin Church, that she may respect and fully appreciate the dignity of Eastern Christians, and accept gratefully the spiritual treasures of which the Eastern Catholic Churches are the bearers, to the benefit of the entire catholic Communion."[14] The pope called upon the Latin Church to "show concretely, far more than in the past, how much she esteems and admires the Christian East and how essential she considers its contribution to the full realization of the Church's universality."[15]

Hence it is not merely a question of the preservation of the Eastern Churches just for their own sake. The traditions and spiritual riches are not the exclusive possession of the Eastern Churches, for they form part of the patrimony of the entire Church of Christ. The sharing of the riches of the faith and traditions of the East nurtures and strengthens the unity in diversity of the Church.

Pope John Paul II indicates how the Eastern Churches can enrich the entire Church. "I listen to the Churches of the East, which I know are living interpreters of the treasure of tradition they preserve. In contemplating it, before my eyes appear elements of great significance for a fuller and more thorough understanding of the Christian experience. These elements are capable of giving a more complete Christian response to the expectations of the men and women of today. Indeed, in comparison to any other culture, the Christian East has a unique and privileged role as the original setting where the Church was born."[16]

Eastern Catholic Churches Today

"Because of religious persecution, war and civil disorders, the twentieth century has witnessed an unprecedented emigration of Eastern Catholics from the lands of their origins. The resulting situation is that the Eastern Churches have become everywhere a minority group, struggling to maintain their apostolic faith and traditions. In the land of their origins they are beset with persecution and sometimes engulfed by an ocean of hostile non-believers. The exercise and preservation of their faith is nearly impossible and difficult at best. In the land of the 'diaspora' they are cultural and ecclesial minorities, struggling to maintain their identity."[17]

Eastern Catholics in the United States of America

The presence of Eastern Catholics in the USA is primarily the result of late nineteenth-century migration from Eastern Europe and the more recent turmoil and upheaval in the Middle East.

Two factors—the lack of their own pastors and the widely scattered nature of the places where they live—have often meant that Eastern Catholics have had to endure long periods without the opportunity of celebrating the holy mysteries according to the liturgical tradition of their own Churches. Moreover, Eastern Catholics have had to face the added difficulty of pressure, both direct and indirect, to abandon their own liturgical celebrations and spiritual heritage and become part of the life of the Latin Church.

Vatican II said that each Eastern Church should "organize its own parishes and hierarchy, where the spiritual good of the faithful requires it."[18] In speaking of this in his recent apostolic letter, John Paul II wrote, "A particular thought goes out to the lands of the diaspora where many faithful of the Eastern Churches who have left their countries of origin are living in a mainly Latin environment."[19] The pope continued, "I particularly urge the Latin Ordinaries in these countries to study attentively, grasp thoroughly and apply faithfully the principles issued by this Holy See concerning ecumenical cooperation and the pastoral care of the faithful of the Eastern Catholic Churches, especially when they lack their own hierarchy."[20]

The Eastern Churches—Spirituality, Liturgy, Law

It is opportune, in the light of these words of Pope John Paul II, to offer some reflections on the Eastern Churches themselves. As Vatican II taught, the autonomous ritual Churches—whether of the East or of the West—are of equal dignity so that none of them is superior to another. Although these Churches differ among themselves in liturgy, law, and spiritual heritage, this variety in no way harms the unity of the Church but rather manifests it.[21]

Pope John Paul II says, "The Christian tradition of the East implies a way of accepting, understanding and living faith in the Lord Jesus. In this sense it is extremely close to the Christian tradition of the West, which is born of and nourished by the same faith. Yet it is legitimately and admirably distinguished from the latter, since Eastern Christians have their own way of perceiving and understanding, and thus an original way of living their relationship with the Saviour."[22]

It is in this spirit that the following brief observations concerning the Eastern Catholic Churches and their experience of faith are offered.

The Trinity in the Life of the Church

> *We have seen the true light. We have received the heavenly Spirit. We have found the true faith. We worship the undivided Trinity for having saved us.*[23]

The history of the Church tells us that the early great theological conflicts about the faith took place in the East. The great ecumenical councils that struggled with the mysteries of the Trinity and the incarnation were held in the eastern half of the Roman Empire while the western half remained relatively untouched. The legacy of this period has left the Eastern Churches with not only a rich theological tradition and the writings of many great church thinkers, but also with a deep sense of the mystery and transcendence of God. As Saint John Chrysostom says, God's "majesty is beyond measure, His wisdom beyond understanding. How then can He Himself be comprehensible?"[24]

For Eastern Catholics, the words of Chrysostom do not remain on a purely intellectual level but permeate their personal and collective spiritual life. However, the feelings of religious awe and transcendence felt by even the most casual participant in an Eastern Catholic liturgy should not be attributed to an agnostic or non-Christian sentiment. The great theologians of the East were also great liturgists and whenever the Liturgy of Saint Basil is celebrated the following prayer is made:

> *Who is able to declare Your mighty love, or to show Your praise in full, and make known Your wonders on all occasions? You, Lord, who are without beginning, unseen, incomprehensible, unchanged, Father of the Lord Jesus Christ who is the image of Your goodness, the seal of Your likeness revealing You, the Father, the Living Word, Life, Sanctification, Power, by whom the Holy Spirit was made manifest, the Spirit of Truth, the Gift of Adoption, the life-giving Power, the Well-Spring of sanctification.*[25]

Therefore, while being deeply conscious of the mystery of God, every member of the Eastern Churches, according to his or her capacity, knows they are called, in the words of Saint Peter, "to become partakers of the divine nature" (2 Pt 1:4). The theological term for this vocation is "Theosis," literally "becoming God," which has become familiar to Western theologians in recent times. For the Eastern Catholic, salvation is not only liberation from sin but an invitation into the inner life of God. All church prayer and action begins and ends within the context of the Most Holy Trinity.

Incarnation

> *At your Baptism in the river Jordan, O Christ, the worship due to the Holy Trinity was made manifest; for the voice of the Father bore you witness, calling you "Beloved Son"; and the Holy Spirit, in the form of a Dove, confirmed this word as steadfast.*[26]

Just as the Eastern Churches have a rich theological and liturgical trinitarian tradition, they have also inherited an equally rich theology of the incarnation. Faith in Christ can never be static and the words of Saint Athanasius—"God became man so that man might become God"—sum up the faith of the simplest member of the faithful.

At Easter the Byzantine and Coptic Churches sing:

> *Christ is risen from the dead. He has crushed death by his death and bestowed life upon those who lay in the tomb.*

For the Eastern Churches, Christ is present and active in the holy mysteries, in his Word, in the person of his ministers and rightly worshiped in his icons. Through all these, he is constantly bestowing divine life. This life is always lived in the light of the Trinity, for as the Gospel of John says, "this is eternal life, that they may know You, the only true God, and Jesus Christ whom You have sent" (Jn 17:3). Jesus is the icon/image of the Father and the One who sends the Holy Spirit into creation.

The Byzantine hymn for Pentecost says:

> *Blessed are You, Christ our God, who have filled the fishermen with wisdom by sending down the Holy Spirit upon them and who, through them, have united the world. Glory to You, O Lover of Mankind!*

Holy Spirit

> *Heavenly King, Advocate, Spirit of Truth, who is everywhere present and fills all things; Treasury of Blessings, Bestower of Life, come and dwell within us; cleanse us from all that defiles us, and, O Good One, save our souls.*[27]

Because of the controversy over the divinity of the Holy Spirit at the time of Saint Basil (c. 330-379), the Eastern Church is aware of the hidden nature of the Spirit, who reveals himself only through what He does in the Church.

A Pentecost hymn describes the work of the Spirit in the following way:

> *The Holy Spirit provides every gift: He inspires prophecy, perfects the priesthood, grants wisdom to the illiterate, makes simple fishermen wise theologians, and establishes the perfect organization of the church.*

No public or private prayer can begin without an invocation of the Holy Spirit, who sanctifies and gives life. The faithful of the Eastern Churches are therefore constantly reminded both in their prayer and sacramental life of the power of the Holy Spirit at work within them.

The Church

The Eastern Churches in the USA live out the mystery of Church not only in a theological but also in a social and historical context. The experiences of many members, both laity and clergy, of these Churches have highlighted and made real certain aspects of the mystery of the Church. Faithful of these Churches have suffered persecution, some-times over many generations, because of their loyalty to the catholicity or universality of Christ's Church.

On the other hand, as most of the members of the Eastern Churches in the USA have memories of migration, the Church has become the focus of community life, and a link with the country of origin and the past.

Nevertheless, there are unique theological, liturgical, and canonical aspects in the way Eastern Catholics live as the Church. The central role of the Eastern patriarchs, and heads of individual Churches, should not be overlooked. As the pope is simultaneously the head of the Latin Church and the Universal Church, it is easy for Latin Catholics to under-estimate the importance of the Eastern patriarchs, as heads of their own individual churches.

The Second Vatican Council took great care to underline the role of the hierarchy of the Eastern Church. "Following the most ancient tradition of the Church, special honor is to be given to the patriarchs of the Eastern Churches, since each is set over his patriarchate as father and head. Therefore this holy council enacts that their rights and priviledges be restored in accordance with the ancient traditions of each church and the decrees of the ecumenical councils."[28]

The Mother of God

What shall we call you, O Lady full of grace?
Heaven, for you have given rise to the Sun of
Righteousness?[29]

Once again the tradition of the Church makes itself felt in the life of the faithful in their devotion to the Mother of God. The Blessed Virgin is never seen as separated from her Divine Son and her role in our salvation. She is always invoked under the title of "Theotokos"—the Mother of God. As Saint John of Damascus wrote, "The term 'Theotokos' contains all the history of divine economy in this world, and the whole mystery of the Incarnation."[30]

The Icon

As the tabernacle of the Covenant held the pres-
ence of God, so do icons show forth the presence
of the One we worship and revere.[31]

No reflection on the Eastern Churches, especially those of the Byzantine tradition, could remain silent on the icon. It is now common to see icons even in the Latin Church, but it must be stressed that they form an integral part not only of the liturgy but also of the theology of the Byzantine Church. The historical background and theological debate that surrounded the icon for more than 100 years (725–842) is similar in intensity to the theological reflection that took place in Western Christianity over the sacrament of the Eucharist. The so-called iconoclast (icon destroyer) controversy provided the Eastern Churches with a variety of precise theological categories and again helped to refine the language and teaching on the mystery of the incarnation. Even those who have read very little Eastern theology will know how central the idea of image is to the sacramentology, systematic theology, and even the moral theology of Eastern Churches.

Liturgy

The Second Vatican Council initiated great changes in the liturgy of the Latin Church. When Latin Catholics attend the liturgy in an Eastern church, they find the celebrations different from their own.

According to Vatican II, "All members of the Eastern Churches should be firmly convinced that they can and ought always preserve their own legitimate liturgical rites and ways of life, and that changes are to be introduced only to forward their own organic development. They themselves are to carry out all these prescriptions with the greatest fidelity. They are to aim always at a more perfect knowledge and practice of their rites, and if they have fallen away due to circumstances of times or persons, they are to strive to return to their ancestral traditions."[32] It is clear from the words of the council that the vision for the Eastern Churches is very different from that proposed for the West, and therefore the success or lack of success should be judged accordingly.

As long as Christians have been able to build their own churches, the area of the altar has been marked out as a special place; sometimes rails have been used, and sometimes steps. In Byzantine churches, the altar is marked off by a screen of icons. This screen developed over many hundreds of years from a simple open screen to a real wall of icons, with doors (also covered with icons) that permit the celebrants to process to and from the altar. To the Latin Catholic, it may seem that the Church is trying to hide the altar from the laity, but the idea that something sacred can be "hidden" behind an icon seems strange to Eastern Catholics. Icons are always the sign of a presence. The icons on the icon-screen are the household of Heaven made up of Christ, the Mother of God, the Angels, and the Saints. Heaven is with us when we celebrate the liturgy and, in a mystical way, actually celebrates the liturgy with us. For Byzantine Catholics, with their long history of theology and devotion, the icon-screen represents a real celebration of the presence of God among us.

Law

The canon law of the Eastern Churches, which was revised after the Second Vatican Council, is contained in the *Code of Canons of the Eastern Churches* which was promulgated by Pope John Paul II on October 18, 1990, and took effect on October 1, 1991. In accordance with this universal legislation, each of the Eastern Catholic Churches can develop its own particular law.

There are some aspects of the discipline of the Eastern Churches that are well known to Latin Catholics, for example, the different discipline in regard to clerical celibacy.

More recently, the existence of married clergy in the East has been used as an argument for making priestly celibacy optional in the West. Questions posed by the Latin Church about its own life and discipline can only be answered by that Church from within its own tradition. The fact that some priests are married and some not has never been a question of debate in the East. As Pope Paul VI noted, "If the legislation of the Eastern Church is different in the matter of discipline with regard to clerical celibacy . . . this is due to the different historical background of that most noble part of the Church, a situation which the Holy Spirit has providentially and supernaturally influenced."[33]

Vatican II, in this matter, stated, "While recommending ecclesiastical celibacy this sacred Council does not by any means aim at changing that contrary discipline which is lawfully practiced in the Eastern Churches. Rather the Council affectionately exhorts all those who have received the priesthood in the married state to persevere in their holy vocation and continue to devote their lives fully and generously to the flock entrusted to them."[34]

The Eastern Churches have a deep reverence for the celibate state as lived by monks and nuns. The episcopate, the fullness of the priesthood, is only bestowed on celibate priests.

The Second Vatican Council sought the restoration of the permanent diaconate. The deacon has always had a central role in the liturgical life of many Eastern Churches, but unfortunately under the influence of the Latin Church, the diaconate came to be seen as a step towards ordination to the priesthood.

The permanent deacon, both in the West and the East, is ordained "not unto the priesthood, but unto the ministry."[35] Nevertheless, the deacon is seen as a member of the hierarchy and not a layman. In the liturgy, the deacon is at the service of the bishop and through him the entire Church. The deacon also has a role in preaching. As the *Code of Canons of the Eastern Churches* states, "Bishops, priests and deacons, each according to the grade of his sacred order, have as their foremost duty the ministry of the Word of God" (*CCEO,* can. 608). Deacons, like priests of the Eastern Churches, may be either celibate or married men.

The Pastoral Care of Eastern Catholics in the USA

In order to consider the pastoral care of Eastern Catholics in the USA, it is necessary to take into account various structures of Eastern Churches, especially the patriarchate and major archiepiscopate.

The Patriarchal Church

This is a Church under the pastoral care of a patriarch. As well as being the eparchial bishop of his own patriarchal eparchy, the patriarch also exercises special jurisdiction over all metropolitans, archeparchs (archbishops), eparchs (bishops), apostolic exarchs (vicars apostolic), and all the clergy and faithful of his Church within the geographical area of his patriarchate. The patriarch's jurisdiction does not extend outside the traditional territory of his patriarchate.

In the USA there are six eparchies and one exarchate of patriarchal or metropolitan *sui iuris* Churches:

The Eparchy of Newton for Melkite Greek Catholics

The Eparchy of Saint Maron in New York for the Maronite Catholics in the Eastern USA

The Eparchy of Saint Thomas in Detroit for Chaldean Catholics

The Eparchy of Our Lady of Lebanon in Los Angeles for Maronite Catholics in the Western USA

The Eparchy of Our Lady of Deliverance in Newark for Syrian Catholics

The Armenian Catholic Exarchate of the USA and Canada

The Romanian Catholic Eparchy of Saint George in Canton, which has its origins from the autonomous Metropolitan Church of Fagaras and Alba Iulia

Major Archiepiscopal Church

A major archbishop is, in almost all respects, identical with a patriarch and has similar rights and privileges.

In the USA there is one metropolitan archeparchy of a major archiepiscopal Church, with three eparchies:

The Archeparchy of Philadelphia for Ukrainian Catholics

The Eparchy of Stamford for Ukrainian Catholics

The Eparchy of Saint Nicholas in Chicago for Ukrainian Catholics

The Eparchy of Saint Josaphat in Parma for Ukrainian Catholics[36]

The Autonomous Metropolitan Church

In the USA there is one autonomous metropolitan Church, that of Ruthenian Byzantine Catholics divided into one archeparchy and three eparchies:

The Archeparchy of Pittsburgh
The Eparchy of Passaic
The Eparchy of Parma
The Eparchy of Van Nuys[37]

Other Eastern Catholic Churches

The other Eastern Churches for a variety of reasons have not yet established an eparchy or an apostolic exarchate in the USA. Some of these Churches—the Russian, Belarusan, Coptic, Ethiopian, Syro-Malabar, and Syro-Malankara—do have one or more priests here in the USA. These priests and their faithful are entrusted to the governance of the local bishop of the Latin Church.

However, members of Eastern Churches who do not have any contact with their own pastors ought to be helped as far as possible to observe their own tradition and customs.

Pope John Paul II expressed a special concern for these Catholics in his apostolic letter *Orientale Lumen*, "Where in the West there are no Eastern priests to look after the faithful of the Eastern Catholic Churches, Latin Ordinaries and their co-workers should see that those faithful grow in the awareness and knowledge of their own tradition, and they should be invited to co-operate actively in the growth of the Christian community by making their own particular contribution."[38]

Sacramental Interecclesial Legislation

When the *Code of Canons for the Eastern Churches* uses the phrase "autonomous ritual church" to designate the Latin Church and the Eastern Catholic Churches, it is evident that laws concerned with the relations between these Churches should no longer be called "interritual" but more appropriately "interecclesial."

In the day-to-day life of the Church, it is usually a question relating to the celebration of the Holy Mysteries of Christian Initiation and Marriage for Eastern Catholics, which require a clear understanding on the part of the minister of the Latin Church.

Membership of Autonomous Ritual Churches

It is not possible simply to be a "Catholic"—a member "at large" of the universal Catholic Church. A person is always a member of a specific autonomous ritual Church and only as such is a person a member of the Catholic Church.[39]

In Baptism, a person is enrolled in an autonomous ritual Church and the Church to which that person belongs is determined by church law. A person, no matter by whom or where or in what liturgical ceremony he or she is baptized, belongs to the autonomous ritual Church to which he or she should belong in accordance with the norms of law. Canons 29-30 of the *Code of Canons of the Eastern Churches* establish the canonical legislation for Eastern Catholics.

From time to time it may become necessary, when it is a question of membership of a Church by reason of Baptism, to clarify to which Church a Catholic belongs. In such cases, the following principles apply:[40]

1. **Baptism of children under the age of fourteen:**

   By virtue of Baptism, a child is enrolled in the Church of the Catholic father or the Church of the mother if only the mother is Catholic or if both parents by agreement freely request it, with due regard for particular laws established by the Apostolic See; these principles also apply in the case of an adoptive father and mother;

   i.   If only one parent is a Catholic, the child belongs to the Church of that parent;

   ii. If born of an unmarried mother, the child belongs to her Church;

   iii. If born of unknown parents, the child belongs to the Church of the legal guardians;

iv. If born of nonbaptized parents the child is to be a member of the Church of the person undertaking the responsibility to educate the child in the Catholic faith.

2. Baptism of children over the age of fourteen:

A person of fourteen years of age or older, who requests Baptism, is free to choose any Church.

The Holy Mysteries of Christian Initiation

Baptism

A priest or deacon of the Latin Church may not baptize a child of Eastern Catholic parents, unless a priest of the parents' Church cannot perform this holy mystery. The following circumstances constitute unavailability of the priest of the Eastern Church, and in such cases a priest or deacon of the Latin Church may baptize the child.

i. The child is in danger of death;

ii. The priest of the Eastern Church is too far away to bring the child to him;

iii. The priest of the Eastern Church cannot come to baptize the child.

If, in these circumstances, a priest or deacon of the Latin Church baptizes the child he must:

i.   State, in his own baptismal register, to which Eastern Church the child belongs;

ii. Send notifications of the baptism to the priest of the Eastern Church;

iii. If there is no priest of the child's Eastern Church in the USA, the registration of the baptism is made only in the parochial register of the Latin Church, but the Eastern Church to which the child belongs must be noted.

Chrismation

In the Eastern Catholic Churches, Chrismation (known in the West as Confirmation) is always received at the time of Baptism. (When there is danger of death, it may be administered later.) If, in the exceptional circumstances as mentioned above, a Latin priest were to baptize a child belonging to an Eastern Church, unless such a priest has the faculties to administer the Holy Mystery of Chrismation and has the permission of the proper pastor to do so, he must not chrismate the child. The child should be chrismated by a priest of his or her own autonomous ritual Church as soon as possible after Baptism.

As many Eastern Catholic children attend Catholic schools
under the control of the Latin Church, it often happens that
they are involved in sacramental preparation programs. It is
at these times that the question of Chrismation arises. As the
Sacrament of Chrismation cannot be repeated, any attempt
to do so is strictly prohibited.

If, at the time of confirmation for the class or group of children in the sacramental program, it is found that a child
belonging to an Eastern Church has not yet received the
holy mystery of Chrismation, the child must then be chrismated in his or her proper autonomous ritual Church.

The Eucharist

It is the normal practice of the Church that Catholics celebrate the Lord's day by participating in the celebration
of the Eucharist in a community of their own Church.
Nevertheless, where there is a diversity of Churches in the
one place, the faithful worthily celebrate the resurrection of
Jesus by attending the Eucharist in any of the autonomous
ritual Churches.

Holy Communion may be received in any Catholic Church.
Since sacramental initiation in the mystery of salvation is
perfected in the reception of the Divine Eucharist, children
of Eastern Catholic Churches who have not received the
Eucharist at the time of their Christian initiation, should

receive their first Holy Communion in their own autonomous Church.

The Holy Mystery of Penance

Catholics may receive absolution from any priest belonging to either the Latin or the Eastern Churches provided he has the faculty to administer the Holy Mystery of Penance. However, priests of the Latin Church hearing the confession of members of Eastern Churches should exercise particular care, as the perception of failing towards God and one's neighbor is deeply formed, and expressed, in terms drawn from one's own liturgical and religious experience.

Priests of the Latin Church need to be aware that the automatic penalties in the law of the Latin Church are not found in that of the Eastern Churches. On the other hand, the practice of "reserved sins" is still retained in the Eastern Churches.

The Holy Mystery of Matrimony

It is at the time of an impending marriage that members of Eastern Churches often come into contact with pastors of the Latin Church.

It is the canonical tradition of Eastern Churches that marriage is to be celebrated before the pastor of the groom unless particular law determines otherwise or a just cause excuses. Unlike the Latin Church, in the Eastern Churches a deacon cannot assist at a marriage.

In the USA, a priest of the Latin Church cannot, without special delegation from the eparch of the Eastern Church, validly bless the marriages of the subjects of that eparch even if celebrated in his parish:

1.   Two Eastern Catholics both of whom belong to the Armenian, Chaldean, Maronite, Melkite, Romanian, Ruthenian, Syrian, or Ukrainian Churches;

2.   An Eastern Catholic belonging to the Armenian, Chaldean, Maronite, Melkite, Romanian, Ruthenian, Syrian, or Ukrainian Churches marrying a baptized person who is not a member of the Catholic Church or an unbaptized person; a bishop of the Latin Church has no authority to permit such a marriage or grant a dispensation for it.

In the USA, a priest of the Latin Church, with the faculty to assist at marriages, may validly bless the following marriages involving Eastern Catholics:

1. Two Eastern Catholics neither of whom belongs to the Armenian, Chaldean, Maronite, Melkite, Romanian, Ruthenian, Syrian, or Ukrainian Churches;

2. An Eastern Catholic who does not belong to the Armenian, Chaldean, Maronite, Melkite, Romanian, Ruthenian, Syrian, or Ukrainian Churches marrying a baptized person who is not a member of the Catholic Church or an unbaptized person.

The marriage between a Latin Catholic and an Eastern Catholic should take place in the Church of the man. Unlike the Latin Church, a deacon in the Eastern Catholic Churches cannot validly assist at a marriage between a man belonging to the Latin Church and a woman belonging to an Eastern Church.

In the case where the groom is a member of the Armenian, Chaldean, Maronite, Melkite, Romanian, Ruthenian, Syrian, or Ukrainian Churches, and the bride is a Latin Catholic, the Eastern Eparch may grant a dispensation so that the marriage may be lawfully celebrated.

When dealing with the faithful of the Eastern Churches, Latin pastors must be aware of the differences in the legislation of the Latin Church and that of the *Code of Canons of the Eastern Churches* in regard to marriage. For example, the impediment of affinity extends in the collateral line to the second degree, that is, prohibiting marriage with one's sister/brother-in-law. The impediment of spiritual relationship is retained in the Eastern Churches so a marriage between a sponsor and the baptized person and the parents of the same is invalid.

The Power to Dispense

Eastern Catholics can only be dispensed by their own eparch. Any dispensation granted by a Latin bishop to the faithful of these Churches is invalid.

Those Eastern Catholics who do not have their own eparchy or exarchate established in the USA are placed under the jurisdiction of the local Latin bishop and may be validly dispensed by him.

Transfer from One Church to Another

In very exceptional circumstances, the Church permits the faithful to transfer their membership from one autonomous ritual Church to another. This is never undertaken lightly and touches upon the deepest relationship between the individual member of the body of Christ, its other members, and the bonds that link us to our Savior. Formerly the power to authorize such a transfer was reserved to the Apostolic

See alone. For Eastern Catholics in the USA, such a transfer may take place on the agreement of the respective bishops. If there is no agreement, the request is submitted to the proper Roman dicastery.

Marriage also provides an opportunity for a person to transfer from one Church to another. An Eastern Catholic wife may transfer to the Church of her husband. A Latin Catholic husband or wife may transfer to the Church of their Eastern spouse at the time of marriage or during the marriage.

Full Communion with the Catholic Church

It can be noted here that for those members of Eastern Orthodox Churches who wish to enter into full communion with the Catholic Church, the Church has never wished to impose any extra burdens. For this reason, where possible, such a person entering into full communion from a non-Catholic Eastern Church should, as Vatican II taught, retain his or her original rite.[41] This leads us to a consideration of ecumenism.

Ecumenism

On May 25, 1995, Pope John Paul II published his encyclical letter *Ut unum sint* in which he said, "The call for

Christian unity made by the Second Vatican Ecumenical Council with such impassioned commitment is finding an ever greater echo in the hearts of believers, especially as the Year 2000 approaches. . . ."[42]

For many Latin Catholics, the mention of Eastern or Oriental Churches is understood as a reference to "the Orthodox Churches," to those Churches of the East that are *not* in full communion with the Catholic Church governed by the successor of Peter and the bishops in communion with him.

For many centuries, the Churches of the East and the West lived out their faith in Christ with little contact with one another but with communion of faith and sacraments. "Human folly and human sinfulness however have at times opposed the unifying purpose of the Holy Spirit and weakened the power of love which overcomes the inherent tensions in ecclesial life. From the beginning of the Church certain rifts came into being. Then more serious dissensions appeared and the Churches in the East found themselves no longer in full communion with the See of Rome or with the Church of the West. Later in the West more profound divisions caused other ecclesial Communities to come into being. These ruptures had to do with doctrinal or disciplinary questions and even the nature of the Church itself."[43] Vatican II acknowledged that "some dissensions have come about 'for which often enough men on both sides were to blame.' "[44]

Gradually, groups and sometimes whole Churches from the East reestablished communion with the See of Rome, while keeping their own traditions. Nevertheless, many groups and Churches in the East continue to be separate from the Universal Church.

Vatican II regarded the Churches not in full communion with the See of Rome with great respect. "These Churches, although separated from us, yet possess true sacraments, above all—by apostolic succession—the priesthood and the Eucharist, whereby they are still joined to us in closest intimacy. . . . Everyone should realize that it is of supreme importance to understand, venerate, preserve and foster the rich liturgical and spiritual heritage of the Eastern Churches in order . . . to bring about reconciliation between Eastern and Western Christians."[45]

Relations between the Catholic Church and the Eastern Orthodox Churches are presently experiencing difficulties. Mutual ignorance and suspicion make any form of real dialogue very difficult. Besides the differences that exist in theology and church practice between the East and West, there is the question of Eastern Catholics. Some Orthodox, aware that some Eastern Catholic Churches came into existence as a result of Catholic missionary activity among their faithful, are of the opinion that these Churches exist today in order to bring Orthodox believers into full communion with the Apostolic See of Rome. In the former communist countries of Central and Eastern Europe, many Eastern Catholic priests, nuns, and lay people suffered death and imprisonment for their faith. The rebirth of these communities in their homeland has caused bitterness among some Orthodox Christians.

The relationship between the Catholic Church and the Orthodox Churches has passed from the dialogue of charity to the theological dialogue of truth. The Eastern Catholic Churches can make an important contribution to this dialogue, and they have a unique role to play in the ecumenical movement.

As the Second Vatican Council states, "The Eastern Churches in communion with the Apostolic See of Rome have the special duty of fostering the unity of all Christians, in particular of Eastern Christians, according to the principles laid down in the decree of this holy council, 'On Ecumenism,' by prayer above all, by their example, by their scrupulous fidelity to the ancient traditions of the East, by better knowledge of each other, by working together, and by a brotherly attitude towards persons and things."[46]

In striving for the unity among all Christians for which Jesus prayed at the Last Supper, the Eastern Catholic Churches will, as Pope John Paul II said, "play a constructive role in the dialogue of love and in the theological dialogue at both the local and international levels, and thus contribute to mutual understanding and the continuing pursuit of full unity."[47]

Notes

1. Vatican Council II, *Lumen Gentium* (LG), no. 1.
2. Paul VI, Opening Allocution to the Second Session of Vatican II, September 29, 1963.
3. LG, no. 5.
4. Cf. Pontifical Council for Promoting Christian Unity, *Directory for the Application of Principles and Norms on Ecumenism,* no. 11.
5. Ibid.
6. Cf. ibid.
7. Ibid., no. 17.
8. Ibid.
9. LG, no. 23.
10. Vatican Council II, *Orientalium Ecclesiarum* (OE), no. 2.
11. Miroslav S. Marusyn, *The Oriental Catholic Churches in the Code of Cannons of the Oriental Churches,* C. Gallagher and Mar Toma Yogam, eds., Rome, 1991, p. 20.
12. LG, no. 23.
13. OE, no. 4.
14. John Paul II, apostolic letter *Orientale Lumen* (OL), no. 21.
15. Ibid.
16. Ibid., no. 5.
17. V. J. Pospishil and J. D. Faris, *The New Latin Code of Canon Law and Eastern Catholics* (CCEC), Diocese of Saint Maron, N.Y., 1984, p. 8.
18. OE, no. 4.
19. OL, no. 26.
20. Ibid.
21. Cf. OE, nos. 2-3.
22. OL, no. 5.

23. Post-Communion Hymn of the Liturgy of Saint John Chrysostom.

24. Migne, *Patrologia Graeca,* 55, 706.

25. Anaphora of Saint Basil.

26. Hymns for the Baptism of Christ.

27. Hymn to the Holy Spirit.

28. OE, no. 9.

29. Prime.

30. *De Fide Orthodoxa,* III, 12.

31. Hymn for the First Sunday of Lent.

32. OE, no. 6.

33. Paul VI, *On Priestly Celibacy,* no. 38.

34. *Presbyterorum Ordinis,* no. 16.

35. Didascalia, II, LG, no. 29.

36. *The Official Catholic Directory.*

37. Ibid.

38. OL, no. 26.

39. Cf. Pospishil and Faris, p. 20.

40. CCEC, canons 29-30.

41. OE, no. 4.

42. John Paul II, encyclical letter *Ut unum sint,* May 25, 1995, no. 1.

43. *Directory for the Application of Principles and Norms on Ecumenism,* no. 18.

44. Ibid.

45. *Unitatis redintegratio,* no. 15.

46. OE, no. 24.

47. *Ut unum sint,* no. 60.